A Perspective of the Difference of Required Knowledge, Skills, and Abilities (KSAs) of Human Resource Professionals in Government Contracting: A Qualitative Study Prospectus

By Dawn D. Boyer, Ph.D.

Book Copyright:	2017© by Dawn D. Boyer, Ph.D.
ISBN Numbers:	ISBN-13: 978-1-948149-03-7 ISBN-10: 1-948149-03-6
Copyright Notice:	2017©: The Author supports copyright. Copyright sparks creativity, encourages diverse viewpoints, and promotes free speech, and creates a vibrant and rich art culture. Thank you for buying an authorized copy of this copyrighted book and for complying with international copyright laws. All copyrights are reserved. No part of this book, including interior design, cover design, icons, and pictures, may be reproduced, or transmitted in any form, by any means (electronic, photocopying, recording, or otherwise) without the prior written permission of the copyright owner. Independent of the author's economic rights, and even after the transfer of the said rights, the author shall have the right to claim authorship of the work and to object to any distortion, modification of, and/or other derogatory action in relation to the said work that could be deemed prejudicial to the author's honor or reputation. No part of this book or images – black and white, or other renditions of images, are to be posted to any social media, Internet, and/or other digital media or platforms without prior written permission of the copyright owner. You are supporting writers and allowing the author to continue to publish books for every other reader to continue to enjoy.
Trademarks:	All brand names, product names, logos, service marks, trademarks or registered trademarks are trademarks of their respective owners.

Author's Business Website	www.DBoyerConsulting.com
Amazon Author Page:	https://www.amazon.com/author/dawnboyer
Review Author's Books:	www.shelfari.com/DawnDeniseBoyer
Facebook Author's Page:	www.facebook.com/DawnBoyerAuthor
Facebook Business Page:	www.Facebook.com/DBoyerConsulting
Google+ Business Page:	https://plus.google.com/112802498128568560150/about?hl=en
LinkedIn	www.linkedin.com/in/DawnBoyer
Twitter:	www.Twitter.com/Dawn_Boyer

Introduction

This book and its content is derived from the Ph.D. cohort, required-curriculum class for Education Foundations 814: Qualitative Research in Education, taught by Dr. Danica G. Hays, in the Fall Semester of 2010.

The project was to create a foundation upon which to design the Ph.D.' student's dissertation, and/or provide a stepping-stone foundation upon which to determine the best research methodologies for the student's final prospectus and dissertation.

The results of the class provided this final project write-up, with literature review and bibliography, and is provided here in it's description entirety.

Introduction

ABSTRACT

This research proposes a heuristic inquiry partnered with a participatory action approach with a post-positivism paradigm to analyze, identify, and study the presumed levels of knowledge, skills, and abilities (KSAs) required to differentiate the two distinct types of business arenas: non-government contracting businesses and government contracting businesses for human resource practitioners (HRPs).

The study recommends interviewing HRPs in a series of one-on-one and using an observation methodology of finding evidence of unique KSAs to the government contracting arena. The participants will be asked to describe their experiences, memories of training, levels of understanding, their opinion of the knowledge, skills, experience, and abilities from their experience to identify those KSAs vital within the government contracting business arena.

This pilot study will be conducted using two research subjects plus observation. The findings will become a benchmark for future and continued studies in a Delphi study to determine those minimum KSA's for industry training purposes, as well as other future study considerations.

A Perspective of the Difference of Required KSA's of Human Resource Professionals in Government Contracting: A Qualitative Study

In the last half-century (pre-2010), the business arena of government contracting agencies providing services and products directly to federal, state, and local area government entities has grown. Unfortunately, the recent economic recession has pressed tighter budget restrictions on all companies, but especially on government contractors' profit margins as the federal government pulls back or cancels contracts (Sherk, 2010). President Barack Obama intends to curtail the government use of external contractors to perform work for the government (Newell, 2010; Obama, 2009), which may not bode well for government contractors. This puts more pressure on HRPs to perform more within their job description and scope, and may expand the need for more KSAs relative to performing their jobs capably.

HRPs working in the federal contracting industry are called upon to perform more tasks and responsibilities that are uniquely different in some cases based on the compliance issues that surround Human Resource (HR) functions in the government contracting industry. HRPs must also know more about the business arena in which they are working. Government Contracting Companies (GCCs) are required to abide by more employment law mandates, executive orders (EO), and contract compliance regulations than non-government contracting businesses (SHRM, 2010; CCH, 2001; Keller, 2010). A HRP is the 'go-to' person for reviewing, understanding, analysis, and advice on compliance information. To truly understand the paradigms for the unique government contracting knowledge, the HR professional also must be in the industry for a few years to experience the business model (SHRM, 2010; HRCI, 2010). These years of experience will help them comprehend the scope and depth of the required laws, EO's, and regulations, as well as the regulatory agencies with oversight (e.g., Office of Federal Contract Compliance Programs [OFCCP]).

Of all the jobs in the United States, there may not be any other that is answerable to, and responsible for tenants of, so many different oversight government agencies, federal legislation, employment law, and presidential executive orders. Just to name a few for non-GCCs: Department of Labor (DOL), Equal Employment Opportunity Commission (EEOC), Occupational Safety and Health Administration (OSHA), Security Exchange Commission (SEC – for Sarbanes-Oxley [SOX] if company is publically traded on stock exchange), US Citizenship and Immigration Services (USCIS), Department of Homeland Security (DHS - immigration), Customs and Border Protection (CBP - immigration), Internal Revenue Service (IRS – taxes), State Tax Agencies (payroll taxes), and the Department of Justice (immigration, work permits and visas). GCCs must also worry about: Office of Federal Contract Compliance Program (OFCCP), Homeland Security – I-9, Social Security (E-Verify), SOX (as a government contractor), and the Department of Defense for security clearances (JPAS), which partners with Department of Homeland Security (DHS) (SHRM, 2010; CCH, 2001; Keller, 2010). Additionally, because of government contracting related finance and accounting practices, HRPs must be cognizant of General Accounting

Practices (GAP) specifically relevant to a niche of knowledge within both HR and the government contracting industry. This ensures unique expenses and charges in the HRPs day-to-day business practices are charged to the correct overhead, general and administrative (G&A) costs, or costs attributable to contract line items for budgetary purposes related to employee expenses, training, and development, per diem charges, and overhead costs (FAR, 2010).

There were approximately 27.5 million businesses in the United States in 2009 (BLS, 2010). As of September 24, 2010, there were 331,557 registered government contractors in the Central Contractor Registry (CCR, 2010). Human resources, training, and labor relations managers and specialists held about 904,900 jobs for all businesses in 2008. If we assume the same percentages (904,900÷27.5M), only .03 percent of 2010 CCR businesses have enough employees to need human resource professionals (HRP) on staff or acting as external consultants. This results in approximately 11,000 human resources practitioners working within the defense industry (SBA, 2010).

The potential reduction of government contractors might force companies to look critically at staff positions for reduction-in-force exercises. This means those HRPs who are not knowledgeable, educated, trained, or have experience in the vital support services related to government contracting may be terminated. Those HRPs with those unique skills and knowledge will be far more desirable and 'hirable' (Elswick, 2001; Mandal, 2008; Meisinger, 2004).

The researcher has been in the HR industry for over 20 years, with half of those years spent working in the government contracting industry. As the researcher moved between non-contracting to the government contracting sectors, the researcher noticed it is a different world of business and work experience(s). Government contractors require huge amounts of specific and unique information, knowledge, skill sets, and education. HRPs in the government contracting industry must know ... beyond ... the basic requirements of those HRPs in 'other' sectors.

The heuristic methodology of research focuses on understanding the "nature, roots, meanings, and essences" of a human experience from the researcher and participants reference point, through descriptions of their experience (Moustakas, 1994). The process begins with self-dialogue, self-search, self-discovery about a problem in one's life experience, but might have a value socially or universally. This entails five to six phases of investigation (depending upon the date of the theory discussion): 1) initial engagement and immersion,[1] 2) incubation, 3) illumination, 4) explication, and 5) creative synthesis. Guided by these stages, the research will reflect backwards upon experiences as a HRP within a GCC regarding a phenomenon to base the selection of participants and constructing the interview questions.

Additionally, the researcher will add a participatory action research (PAR) or what is sometimes referred to as action research (AR) methodology to the study to blend the research into a rich analysis of information. The PAR method's goals are to be useful, employ diverse methods, and use collaboration (Stoecker, 2005, p. 30) while it seeks to answer three questions: 1) who is the community, 2) is there conflict or cooperation involved, and could the method be biased in terms of the present or absent voices in the collaborative process? Using six phases of the process the goal is to provide an improvement to a process or policy. Those six phases are: 1) a current theory, research, or practice is in place, 2) learning is

---

[1] *Depending upon the date and the theory author, initial engagement and immersion may be considered one and the same or two separate stages (Moustakas, 1994, p.27; Patton, 2002, p. 486)*

part of the culture, 3) partnerships are formed, 4) there is a goal or problem identification, 5) there is formative research, and 6) there is a culture specific theory or model (Stoecker, 2005).

This heuristic inquiry study is significant to the researcher because of past experiences (*initial engagement & immersion*) in which the researcher was hired as a HRP for a GCC with the promise of training that never materialized. The personal lesson learned was a training curriculum focused on the variance of required HR knowledge would have tremendously lessoned the steep learning curve, as well as problematic issues of understanding the industry overall. It was a sharp learning curve for which the researcher wasn't prepared, but now that factors of experience and knowledge have been identified as missing at the time, it's easy to recognize the knowledge delta (*incubation*). While working in the government contracting companies, the research worked alongside those in the same situation, and formed friendships and partnerships (*collaboration*) to get through knowledge and learning situations for which this group (*community*) identified as lacking for KSAs at the time. There were orientations to the GCCs initially (*learning the culture*), but it was up to the individuals to work with each other (*forming partnerships*) to reach work related objectives *(goal setting or problem identification)*.

There are a few organizations that provide training and development, as well as certifications to HRPs (e.g., SHRM's PHR, SPHR, GPHR, etc.), they are certifications to the general human resources field versus unique to the government contracting industry (SHRM, 2010; CEBS, 2010).

A qualitative study on this problem will provide a rich source of data from participants which are more illustrative of what information they don't know, do remember, and/or might have been exposed to within their roles as HRPs working for GCCs. The researcher's experience, as part of the heuristic tradition of data collection methodology can provide a third set of data experience to triangulate the information from the subjects' data and observation data to collect a defensible report of baseline information from which to create a set of learning objectives for those seeking entry into levels within the organization (GCCs) requiring a cognitive awareness of the industry.

Purpose

The purpose of this participatory action research study is twofold: (a) to explore the experiences of HRPs in GCCs, and (b) to attempt (via those interviews focusing on the interviewee's background and experience) to identify the delta of information, KSAs between the two types of HRPs in two distinct business arenas – non-GCCs and GCCs. The discussions should result in identification of a set of unique KSAs related to employment laws, mandates, regulations, and industry specific knowledge within that business arena. Once identified, the result would be a unique collection of data that could be marketed by learning institutions or training companies focusing on providing training and development (T&D) to that demographic niche market.

The following research questions will guide this study: (a) are there identifiable KSAs for HRPs to perform capably within a general business environment, and (b) are there identifiable unique and additional KSAs for HRPs to perform capably within the government contracting business environment.

Research Paradigms and Tradition

This study will be conducted utilizing a 'post-positivism' paradigm. Ontologically, the study is based on the belief there are universal processes, knowledge, skill sets, and abilities (KSAs) employed to perform as a HRP within any business setting. The researcher acknowledges there will be a variety of degrees for each subjects' viewpoint of the KSAs needed to perform capably in the HRP position. Epistemologically, while those KSAs are observable (positivism), and can be described, they can also be directly or indirectly measured (post-positivism). In this research study, there will be an axiological level of influence on the data and subject matter based on the researchers work history within the human resources field, as well as within the GCC venue. Rhetorically, the researcher will be speaking to the report and writing the information in the third person (voice) to maintain some semblance of neutrality, but because this is a blended study using a heuristic approach, some bias and prejudice may be evident in the final data report.

The researcher will be able to obtain ontological data that is observable, measurable, real, with controllable standards within a universal truth, which would be a baseline of KSA required for a capable HRP to practice. There is also the recognition 100% identification of all the data and variables will not occur, since some businesses don't require all KSAs. Although variables affecting performance may not be identified, major themes may be discovered (Campbell & Russo, 1999; Patton, 2002). This formative evaluation study will ascertain the participant's understanding of best business practices in the human resources field, where unique knowledge, education, experience, and skill sets (KSA's) might be recognized as minimum standards for capabilities in this type of industrial setting. The evaluation of the data results will describe a baseline for those required KSA's. This evaluative study will be used inductively to identify general themes emerging from the discussions and data collection focusing on effective practices across multiple types of GCC business models (services or products sold to federal, state, or local governments). These evaluations will result in lessons learned for better benchmarking practices and further analysis (Patton, 1997).

Research Question(s) and Sub-Question(s)

This blended research study using heuristic and participatory action research will attempt to identify specific knowledge, skills, or abilities (KSAs) cognitively vital to human resource practitioners (HRPs) within a government contracting company (GCC). The theories the researcher proposes to hypothesize are:

H1: There are specific/unique KSAs required of HRPs working in GCCs vital for job performance; (these specific/unique KSAs are not required of HRPs working in non-GCCs).

H2: The specific/unique KSAs required of HRPs working within GCCs have created a niche community of workers within a job (title & level) who collaboratively and cooperatively share information to perform better for their organization.

H3: Identifying the KSAs unique to the GCC HRPs will provide a baseline for additional research, training/development, and learning objectives for those aiming for careers within the GCCs business arena.

Operationalized Variables

The focus of the study is to identify KSA elements demonstrating strengths and weaknesses of specific personnel factors. The researcher seeks recommendations for improvement, related to the subject matter, from the subjects.

The primary target audience for the report data conclusions of this study is HRPs, as well as executives (working for GCCs) who need to understand the HRPs job tasks and responsibilities for hiring or promotional purposes relative to cognitive and minimum capabilities for the positions. The goal is to uncover common areas of participants' experiences to explore and improve the focus and scope of knowledge. The researcher hopes to ascertain the professional impact of these KSAs related to cognitive expectations of the job, as well as focus on learning objectives and methods to reach those KSAs. HRPs will be interviewed to determine their perspectives on their education, work experiences, KSAs related to their positions within a GCC. This study should uncover perceptual and actual KSAs required, to improve experiences and career development of this niche demographic.

The research findings may improve HRPs performance through suggested formal or informal educational programs, training modules, mentoring experiences, and skills necessary in this unique business arena. Once the study is completed, the results will be limited in circulation until the data results are published as part of a follow-on study within a dissertation program.

Method

Participants and Procedure: In the pilot study the participants are the researcher and two HRP peers. For the full qualitative study, the recommendation would be approximately 10-15 participants in the human resources field, with participants currently in HRP roles from administrative support up to director level, as well as in small (50-100 employees), mid-sized (100-500), and large companies (500+). An attempt would be made to diversify for formal education and ethic background to truly make this a well-rounded research.

The procedure would entail one-on-one interviews, either face-to-face or via teleconference. Those not meeting in person with the researcher would be sent a package with the mind-map drawn out with all the generalist areas of human resource practice and a short introduction about the study, what the research goals are, and what is to be accomplished with the study. There would be an informed consent, as well as notification there is no right or wrong answer; their viewpoint is what is sought.

Research Team: The researcher in this study is an individual. For the full study, the recommendation is for a team of HRPs outside and within the GCC community is used for bracketing the assumptions of HRP KSAs within a GCC. Those team members outside the GCC can ask questions and confirm terms not used in the business arena, while those within can confirm definitions or provide validity to material.

Interview Protocol: The HRP participants will be asked to meet with the researcher, and the researcher will follow a semi-structured interview protocol. The time frame of this study will be to perform a set of meetings with the targeted subjects within a set time-period with one-on-one interviews, and record the informal session while the data is discussed in a casual setting.

Participants will be shown a mind map with a layout of the various and main concerns of KSA related to human resources which may fall into the realm of knowledge needed by a HRP working for a GCC. Once the participants understand the various topics to be covered, the discussion on each subheading will explore if any topics were omitted and need to be added to the discussion. There will be no grading or scale of measurement associated with this discussion of the mind map topics. The type and degree of control for the data collection will be naturalistic, where a naturalistic inquiry strategy would be the best methodology, followed by a deductive content analysis of the data collected. The validity of the data will be confirmed by triangulating multiple sources and types of data from the individual resources (subjects).

The next step in the interview will be to go through a list of terms, which have been gathered by the researcher and an external source. The researcher will read the term, and ask the participant if they are familiar with the term, if so, what is the definition, and what, if any, relationship is there between the term and knowledge that a HRP needs as a practitioner with a GCC. The data to be collected will be qualitative in a sense – information easily identifiable and understood by the subjects – to add to the knowledge base of specific topics.

Once the interviews have taken place, coding will begin for major and minor themes. Member checking[2] will be followed by research team code assistance, suggestions, and discussion. After the member-check and research team discussion, re-coding and expansion of themes and sub-themes will take place.

There will be only one primary researcher involved in the data collection, but class peers (reviewing team) are involved in the review of the questions and the proposal, as well as the class instructor. There will be minimum personnel materials, and publishing or reporting costs. The largest cost will be in the man-hours used to transcribe the session data.

Participants: Since this study is a blend of heuristic inquiry and participatory action research, one of the participants is the researcher. Because the researcher has information, knowledge, skills, and abilities from past work experience, this is used as one part of the data to be triangulated. The participatory action research objective is to take the researcher and peers' knowledge, reflect on experiences in a niche job

---

[2] *A review of interview data with participants.*

within a niche field and industry and determine what makes those experiences, knowledge, and skills (and abilities) so specific and vital to that job a special training curriculum could be designed for it.

Demographics: Access to this group of participants (other than the researcher) will be peers in GCCs, easily accessible within a social group or trade organization, a work history within human resources (circa five years or more, so thus can be considered subject matter experts [SME]), a work history within a GCC (circa five years or more, thus an assumed SME), and willing to participate in the study. This is a purposeful sample from a homogenous group of subjects (who work within a specific business sector), who are purposefully random (but data rich), and where data results are comprehensive (all have a voice in the data collection).

The phenomenon of the case will be to focus on a critical set of subjects who have experience (SMEs) in this unique type of employment situation (Yoon & Sundar, 2010), the criterion they fulfill is: 1) they are HRPs, 2) having worked in GCCs, and 3) they will be able to confirm or argue factors from the terms and data provided. Participants will sign an informed consent form.

To ensure a comprehensive, homogenous, and rich source of data, the researcher will seek out approximately 10-15 participants who currently work within government contracting companies (at least five years) and are in the mid- to high-level management. This demographic will ensure a rich source of data, based on years of experience and exposure to the business arena, and whom may also have a rich cross-exposure to other departments within the organization such as contracts, finance, proposals and bids, and the executives, thus have more exposure to a more varied vocabulary of terms and experiences from the HR viewpoint.

Researcher / Researcher's Team

Bias: The researcher does have a bias in the form of a reflective and preconceived opinion there is a difference in the KSAs of HRPs who work outside the GCC business arena and those who work within a GCC business environment. This bias comes from personal experience working as a HRP moving from a non-GCC to a GCC business a little over a decade from the date of this study. The move confounded the researcher – there were so many business and GCC-related policies, principles, new regulations, training, development, etc. – it was overwhelming. Watching new hires as they were brought into the human resources department demonstrated some type of industry and job related training was critically needed to avoid repeatedly occurring, time-consuming, self-esteem reducing, and time-consuming mistakes.

    The researcher continued to build knowledge and skills over the decade by attending school, taking training classes, and webinars, as well as attending conferences and symposiums related to human resources, business, and government contracting. As the researcher's career and education progressed and vertical (promotional) movements achieved, it became apparent to the researcher that HRPs within a GCC were not always fully cognizant of vitally related KSAs needed to perform their job capably outside of rote tasks and responsibilities. This was obvious for those new to the GCC arena. There seemed to be a thematic string of understanding learned by the researcher through observation and reflection. This understanding resulted in an exploratory idea to find out 'what was missing' in most HRP training related directly to development of human resources practitioners' knowledge, skills, and abilities within government contracting companies. If 'what was missing' was compiled into one report, then that data could be used as a springboard to develop an appropriate curriculum for training and development.

Assumptions: The assumptions for this heuristic inquiry study are two-fold – those of the research team and those of the participants. For the researcher and team, the assumptions are they have enough knowledge of the KSAs to be able to credibly recognize, define, and document those themes and topics related to GCCs and the human resources field of knowledge. There is also the assumption that coding the interview and observation data will result in specific and general themes or threads that can be converted to a reliable and valid reporting of the data upon which to base a curriculum design. There is an assumption the researcher's (or team's) knowledge is equal to the participants so data can be recognized as relevant. Another assumption is data collected and reported upon can be used in curriculum development.

An assumption in the pilot study was the participants had a rich exposure to HR terms, definitions, and culture within a GCC, and they would know as much as a mid-level HR manager or supervisor. For the pilot study participants, the assumption is they have relevant experience in both human resources, as well as the government contracting business arena, and have enough experience to have reached some level of competency, capability, and KSAs to know what the researcher is discussing in the interviews. To increase the strength of the study, participants will need to be of a higher than clerical or administrative level position; preferably mid- to high-level HR supervisor or manager.

Information provided by the participants will assist in triangulation of data by the telling (*story relating*) provided during interviews. Their narratives *(verification of core data)* will provide explanation of the breadth and depth of their knowledge, and potentially what might have been encountered in their GCC positions, and what might be relevant based on the type of GCC (or size).

Assumptions for the participatory action research (PAR) study for the researcher are there is a delta, gap, misunderstanding, or non-existence of a set-of-knowledge that could empower HRPs working in GCCs. The researcher assumes some (or many) HRPs hired into GCCs are knowledgeable of general HR practices, but might not be cognizant of standard or unique business practices for GCCs (finance, contracts, specialized recruiting, ethics, GCC-specific laws, regulations, or executive orders, etc.). The assumption is there is a need for a 'change agent' which provides an action plan to enable those HRPs to become more knowledgeable, skilled, and capable to perform their jobs with a greater return on investment (ROI) by their employer. The additional assumption for the PAR is participants recognize they do not have the KSAs, and desire those additional KSAs to perform better in a HRP position for a GCC.

Data Sources

The methodology of this research study will be via: 1) self-reflection of the researcher's past-experience, 2) one-on-one interviews with other HRPs, and 3) observation of data found in published HRP journals, books, texts, and study guides. Observation of data will identify 'living'[3] documents of information

---

[3] Defined as constantly changing per legislation, new laws going into effect, etc., where the content, definitions, and wording may change at various rates and times.

relative to law, regulations, and policies via government websites, brochures, and other publically available documents as it relates to the HRP KSAs. These various methods of collecting data will aim at finding consensus for the data from the individuals and the group members to validate the information gathered and triangulate data collected in the preliminary study.

The first unit of analysis will be knowledge the researcher has gained in over twenty years of practice in the human resources field in positions from generalist, specialist, recruiter, and director within three different GCCs. While the information and knowledge can not be encapsulated into a precise summary for this study, suffice it to say researcher has the basis upon which to draw the mind-map, and gather the initial definitions and words upon which to interview peer HRPs. While this may be identified as a bias or weakness, the information rich sampling and researcher's own knowledge would provide a baseline of information about issues of central importance to the study.

The second unit of analysis will be HRPs who have worked within the human resources industry for at least five years and approximately five years within the government contracting business arena. These HRPs have unique viewpoints and the ability to identify the differences between the corporate business world and operations in government contracting, as well as insights to the differences in HRP best practices in both worlds. The study will look at HR components, but concentrate only on those analytical units differentiated between the two different types of business practices. This follows the qualitative methodology of purposeful sampling, only capturing data from those who have a rich history of experience in the narrowly defined components.

The third unit of data analysis will be public documentation of employment law, compliance law and regulations, executive orders, specific regulatory policy from government agencies and departments noted in the first section of this prospectus.

To define the sampling overall, it would be identified as a blend of a) intensity sampling (information rich cases focusing on phenomenon intensity), (b) homogenous sampling (focusing on similar backgrounds and experiences, and (c) criterion sampling (meeting pre-determined criterion of importance) (Patton, 2002). Opportunistic and convenience sampling may occur if there is an opportunity to identify a member of a group who knows and understands the objectives of the study and can contribute to the information sought, e.g., finance managers, proposal manages, contract managers, who have worked in the government contracting business arena and have insight to the roles and responsibilities of human resource managers.

Interviews: There are business topics or issues within the human resources field HRPs would need to understand, have an education in, and have the experience to handle. There are multiple organizations, which provide certifications, as well as secondary level schools providing undergrad or graduate level degrees in HR.

The researcher created a 'mind-map' to illustrate various departments or themes related to unique, but standardized, topics HRPs would be responsible for within a GCC. The number of interviews total were one each participant, plus a 'member-check' accomplished by e-mailing the participant the copy of the transcript to perform a review and commentary back to the researcher for any clarifications or miscommunications. Participants declined to return or comment on the interviews by noted deadline, thus the researcher assumes the transcriptions were verbatim, and approved by the participants.

The main topics of generalization discusses with the participants were:

1) employment law compliance
2) recruiting, new hires, and orientation
3) benefits and compensation
4) ethics, related finance compliance, and
5) general training and development.
6) In addition to general issues, a HRP in a GCC would also need to know specialty information related to:
7) federal compliance for ethics (Sarbanes-Oxley [SOX])
8) federal contractor fraud, waste, and abuse
9) time-sheet training and hours worked
10) security DoD clearances (Joint Personnel Adjudication System – JPAS)
11) special training and development related to ethics (human trafficking for employees traveling outside the continental United States (CONUS), and
12) Federal Acquisition Regulation (FAR) and General Services Administration (GSA) contract law.

The researcher's questions will be centered specifically upon these topics and what 'above-and-beyond' the first set of issues would a HRP in a GCC need to know that is vitally important to know that a non-GCC HRP would not need. Thematic words will be read to participants to enable and prompt discussion, definitions, and thoughts as to how these words fit into the HRP practice for everyday KSAs within a GCC:

- 1st class airfare
- ACO – authorized contracting officer
- ACRNs – Accounting Classification Reference Number
- Advertising
- Alcoholic beverages
- Approval matrix
- Bids & Proposals
- CAS – Contract Administration Services
- CLINs – Contract Line Item Number
- CONUS – Continental US
- Daily time keeping
- Davis-Bacon act
- DCAA – Defense Contracting Audit Agency
- DCAA floor checks
- DCAAM – Defense Contract Audit Agency Manual
- DCAAP – Defense Contract Audit Agency Pamphlet
- DCMA – Defense Contract Management Agency
- Delivery Orders
- DFAS – Defense Finance & Accounting Service (DoD)

- Direct vs. Indirect (costs to contract)
- Donations
- Drug screening
- DSS – DLA (Defense Logistics Agency) Support Services
- Entertainment (allowable vs. unallowable)
- Ethics training
- FAR – Federal Acquisition Regulation
- Gifts
- Interest expense
- JTR – Joint Travel Regulation
- Labor Categories – Job Classifications
- Lowest airfare
- OCONUS – Out of the Continental US
- Overtime (OT) - premium pay
- Overhead vs. General & Administrative G&A (expenses)
- Parties (allowable / unallowable expense)
- Penalties
- Per Diem rates
- Period of Performance
- Policies & Procedures
- Prevailing wages
- Project Accounting
- Promotions
- Proper audit trails
- SCA – Service Contract Act
- Security badges
- Security clearances
- SLINs - Sub-Line Item Numbers
- Timesheet changes
- Timesheet deadlines
- Total time accounting
- Travel
- Unallowable costs

Observations: The researcher has access to multiple sources for obtaining reliable and valid data related to laws, regulations, and executive orders from multiple government agencies, departments, and organizations, as well as trade organizations which publish layman's guides, interpretations, and discussion boards and forums.

Sequence of Data Collection: Data was collected in the order of 1) researcher's reflections, ideas, and typed research paper with literature review, 2) participant interview number one, 3) participant interview number one, and 4) observation by collection of printed data and documentation. The observation could have occurred at any point in the study, even before the researcher's reflections, because it was stand-alone, but critical for triangulation.

Additional Actions for Research Study from Pilot Study Reflections: Relying upon the pilot study's observations and reflections, the researcher would make changes in the IRB approved, full-research study project. The researcher would reach out to approximately 10 to 15 participants to fully gain a more diverse variety of responses from the HR community. An assumption in the pilot study was the participants had a rich exposure to HR terms, definitions, and culture within a GCC. The assumption was proven untrue in the pilot study with the two participants, and a broader assumption might be interpreted to indicate the level of participant in the larger research study should concentrate on mid-level HR supervisors or managers and above.

Data Analysis

The analysis started with Moustakas' initial *engagement* and *immersion* (1990, p. 28) which focuses on exploring the experience of the 'question,' dialoging with peers (*participant selection*) who were assumed to be SMEs (Sandelowski, 1986, p. 31), and while there was a mind-map to guide discussion and a list of words to define, and the conversation was open where the voice of the participants was as important as the researcher's. *Data* was *collected* via transcribed interviews with peers, observation of documents, and the researcher's own knowledge and interaction (within the interviews). There was an *incubation* period for the researcher to reflect on the data, discuss with research team, and peers, and a better understanding evolved, partnered with the sorting, editing, coding, and re-coding of the data. The coding provided an *illumination* for the central themes in the phenomenon of the study (Moustakas, 1990, p. 29) where new meanings for the methodology of data collection, the data itself, and the definitions emerged. *Creative synthesis* allows the researcher to expand or contract the data to more specifically to the next level of study and research data, and/or looking for more triangulating data via SME interviews or observation(s).

The researcher was integrated into the (heuristic) participant experience as a SME, as well as a pivotal *change agent* to seek the knowledge for compartmentalization to specific topics to use as baseline for process improvement (PAR) as the central principal of the pilot research study. Once the data was collected, the analysis began by sorting, editing, distilling the researcher's and the participants' knowledge and experience, and then matching it to observation data. Some of the coding became superfluous and deleted as non-unique in the coding book(s). The data was input to a spreadsheet from 'indexed' codes in the transcriptions, reduced to general themes, and then further reduced to larger general themes and summarization. This took several passes to organize the text, and code and re-code, while the researcher studied the field and reflected on each previous action. Eventually, the researcher could identify themes and patterns, which illuminated the research project's overall significance. This points back to the heuristic illumination and explication (Moustakas, 1990), while also providing a program evaluation for future study and research.

What emerged or developed was a main narrative (theory) from the creative synthesis (Moustakas, 1990); for which *action* can be taken to present data to create policy, procedure, education, or training changes for learners. While this post-positivism outcome may never reach 100% consensus because there is a variable of size of company, service or product produced, number of employees or HRPs in the organization, it might get close enough to a conceivable *truth* to develop a curriculum for a viable, reliable, and valid learning experience.

Strategies for Trustworthiness

The researcher made every effort to show non-malfeasance (avoid harm, informed consent), beneficence (maximizing benefits for 'community'), justice (groups are not harmed nor given advantage over another), fidelity (maintaining trust, long-term), and veracity (truthfulness in all dealings), in the role of the Researcher (relationship(s) with participants). Informed consent forms were obtained, the study was discussed thoroughly with the participants, all observable data was collected from government public domain sites, as well as published books and journals, which were cited appropriately. The participants were provided verbatim transcripts to review for corrections, edits, or further explanation. In the implementation of the study, there was an order of strategies and a research team was consulted to avoid bias. Date reporting triangulated facts and definition. Confidentiality protected participants. In this heuristic study, the researcher identified previous experiences with participants. Data was reported with accuracy, truthfulness, and comprehensiveness (verbatim transcriptions).

Pilot Study

Method: The researcher interviewed two participants for approximately one hour and later transcribed the data verbatim. The interview consisted of showing the participants a mind-map with a theoretical layout of a HRPs tasks and responsibilities within a GCC. The researcher was also considered a participant, as used personal experiences to explore and expand upon the dialog during the interviews.

Pilot Study Results: The pilot study resulted in approximately fourteen sub-themes for KSAs related to HRP practice within GCCs. Those themes (in alpha order) were: 1) Accounting, contract specific; 2) Accounting, per diem, government rates; 3) Auditing and accounting; 4) Benefits and compensation; 5) Company internal policies; 6) Contract job requirements; 7) Contract oversight; 8) Contract requirements; 9) Contracting – government (genl.); 10) EEOC, AAP, and compensation; 11) Ethics; 12) General HR; 13) Government contracting requirements; and 14) Legal, regulatory, and executive orders. Of these, one through three might be combined; six through nine plus thirteen may be combined, and ten and fourteen may also be combined; to result in seven main issues HRPs in GCCs must be cognizant of, knowledgeable about, and skilled in administrative support. This boils down to the following themes standing out in this pilot research study: Accounting, Benefits & Comp, Company Policies, Contract related Issues, Law, Ethics, and General HR related to GCC activities.

Potential Results Based on Pilot Study: Relating back to the questions for this research study to answer, theories H1-H3, this shows (H1) there are specific and unique KSAs required of HRPs working within GCCs, which are not required of HRPs working in non-GCC organizations. The unique KSAs (H2) required of HRPs working within GCCs have created a niche community with information necessary to perform better for their

GCC organization. There was identified KSAs unique to GCC HRPs, which provides a baseline for research, training and development, and learning objectives for those aiming for careers within the GCCs business arena.

How Study Contributes to the Human Resources Field: This study is significant because there currently is no unique training or development in existence for this niche market of workers who must learn via On-The-Job-Training (OJT), from peers or mentors, or the school of hard knocks or through negative experiences (failures, mistakes, etc.). The core KSAs for HRPs is generalized, thus developing a specialized training and development program that focuses on learning more about government contracting, related issues, and specialized KSAs pivotal to minimally performing the tasks and responsibilities at a certain level of leadership would provide a path of new career and promotional opportunities for thousands of HRPs.

Potential Limitations: The total limitations of the study results may not be known, but some exist. Limitations to the study is that the pilot study was limited to lower level experienced HRPs, and their work history may not have been exposed to the type of information that higher-level leadership may have. The researcher may not have gathered all the appropriate terminologies, definitions, or left out issues from the original mind-map for interview discussion(s).

Limitations to future use of the study: HRPs may not feel information related to any aspect of the GCCs main business is relevant to their tasks and duties outside the HR department. Executives in GCCs may not want HRPs to break across the departmental 'silos' to have input into other sectors of business. Mid-level to higher managers may already have the necessary HR knowledge to perform in lieu of HRPs or there may not be a designated HRP within the company (clerical performs minimal HR-related functions). HRPs may not want to learn about government contracting.

Potential Ethical Issues: The researcher is unaware of any ethical issues or professional and cultural concerns related to the outcomes of this pilot research study.

Conclusion:

The researcher's awareness of the topic issues shared in commonality with HRPs and GCCs is unique, there is a niche for a community which could benefit from this specific knowledge (KSAs), and there is an exciting opportunity to be expanded in future research for training and development relative to this niche job market.

APPENDIX

APPENDIX A

Old Dominion University
Informed Consent Form

The following is the example of the wording of the Informed Consent Forms provided to study participants. Personal point of contact information has been deleted for privacy.

PROJECT TITLE

A Perspective of the Difference of Required KSA's of Human Resource Professionals in Government Contracting: A Qualitative Study

INTRODUCTION

The purposes of this form are to give you information that may affect your decision whether to say YES or NO to participation in this research, and to record the consent of those who say YES.
Research Study: A Perspective of The Difference of Required Ksa's Of Human Resource Professionals in Government Contracting: A Qualitative Study
Research conducted in a private home of researcher.

RESEARCHER(S)

Dawn D. Boyer, PhD Student, Darden College of Education, investigation for Foundations 814, Qualitative Research, Instructor: Dr. Danica Hays

DESCRIPTION OF RESEARCH STUDY

This research proposes a participatory action approach with a post-positivism paradigm to analyze, identify, and study the differences in the levels of knowledge, skills, and abilities (aptitudes) that are required in the two distinct types of business arenas: non-government contracting businesses and government contracting businesses. The study recommends interviewing human resource professionals in a series of one-on-one and a focus group session. The participants will be asked to describe their experiences, training, levels of understanding, knowledge required, skills and experience, and abilities outside the non-government business arena to identify those KSA's vital within the government contracting business arena compared to a non-governmental contract business. This pilot study will be conducted using two or three research subjects. The findings will become a benchmark for future and continued studies in a Delphi study to determine those minimum KSA's for industry training purposes, as well as other future study considerations.

EXCLUSIONARY CRITERIA

NA

RISKS AND BENEFITS

RISKS: If you decide to participate in this study, then you may face zero risk. And, as with any research, there is some possibility that you may be subject to risks that have not yet been identified.

BENEFITS: The main benefit to you for participating in this study is learning about what others feel are important KSA's in the HR arena in a government contracting business field.

COSTS AND PAYMENTS

The researchers want your decision about participating in this study to be absolutely voluntary. Yet they recognize that your participation may pose some inconvenience. To defray your costs, you will receive a lunch help defray incidental expenses associated with participation.

NEW INFORMATION

If the researchers find new information during this study that would reasonably change your decision about participating, then they will give it to you.

CONFIDENTIALITY

The researchers will take reasonable steps to keep private information, such as questionnaires, employment history confidential. [If applicable: The researcher will remove identifiers from the information, destroy tapes, store information in a locked filing cabinet prior to its processing. The results of this study may be used in reports, presentations, and publications; but the researcher will not identify you. Of course, your records may be subpoenaed by court order or inspected by government bodies with oversight authority.

WITHDRAWAL PRIVILEGE

It is OK for you to say NO. Even if you say YES now, you are free to say NO later, and walk away or withdraw from the study at any time. If applicable, your decision will not affect your relationship with Old Dominion University, or otherwise cause a loss of benefits to which you might otherwise be entitled. The researchers reserve the right to withdraw your participation in this study, at any time, if they observe potential problems with your continued participation.

COMPENSATION FOR ILLNESS AND INJURY

If you say YES, then your consent in this document does not waive any of your legal rights. However, in the event of any harm, illness, medical issues arising from this study, neither Old Dominion University nor the researchers are able to give you any money, insurance coverage, free medical care, or any other compensation for such injury.

In the event that you suffer injury as a result of participation in any research project, you may contact Dawn Boyer or the current IRB chair, at (XXX) XXX-XXX, at Old Dominion University, who will be glad to review the matter with you.

VOLUNTARY CONSENT

By signing this form, you are saying several things. You are saying that you have read this form or have had it read to you, that you are satisfied that you understand this form, the research study, and its risks and benefits.

The researchers should have answered any questions you may have had about the research. If you have any questions later on, then the researchers should be able to answer them:

Dawn Boyer, Cell: (XXX) XXX-XXXX

If at any time you feel pressured to participate, or if you have any questions about your rights or this form, then you should call the current IRB chair, at (XXX) XXX-XXX, or the Old Dominion University Office of Research, at 757 683 3460.

And importantly, by signing below, you are telling the researcher YES, that you agree to participate in this study. The researcher should give you a copy of this form for your records.

Subject's Printed Name & Signature
Date

Parent/Legally Authorized Representative's Printed Name/Signature
Date

Witness' Printed Name & Signature (if Applicable)
Date

INVESTIGATOR'S STATEMENT

I certify that I have explained to this subject the nature and purpose of this research, including benefits, risks, costs, and any experimental procedures. I have described the rights and protections afforded to human subjects and have done nothing to pressure, coerce, or falsely entice this subject into participating. I am aware of my obligations under state and federal laws, and promise compliance. I have answered the subject's questions and have encouraged him/her to ask additional questions at any time during the course of this study. I have witnessed the above signature(s) on this consent form.

Investigator's Printed Name & Signature

Date

APPENDIX B

CODES

The following codes were identified during the research participant's discussions, interviews, surveys, and other communications under the umbrella of the qualitative research project by the Ph.D. student.

Topic (Code) With Interview "specific" Page	Interview #	CODE MAIN THEMES	SECONDARY MAIN THEMES	NOTES
Defense Finance Accounting System (DFAS), 14	B	Benefits and Compensation	Accounting, Contract Specific	
allowable, 16, 19, 20	B	Compliance (law, regulatory, finance)	Accounting, Contract Specific	
direct, 14, 19	B	Compliance (law, regulatory, finance)	Accounting, Contract Specific	
overhead, 14, 19	B	Compliance (law, regulatory, finance)	Accounting, Contract Specific	
penalties, 19	B	Compliance (law, regulatory, finance)	Accounting, Contract Specific	
per diem rates, 20	B	Compliance (law, regulatory, finance)	Accounting, Contract Specific	
period of performance, 20	B	Government Contracting (DoD)	Accounting, Contract Specific	

Topic (Code) With Interview "specific" Page	Interview #	CODE MAIN THEMES	SECONDARY MAIN THEMES	NOTES
airfare, 10, 18	B	Compliance (law, regulatory, finance)	Accounting, Per Diem, Gov. Rates	
Joint Travel Regulation, 17	B	Compliance (law, regulatory, finance)	Accounting, Per Diem, Gov. Rates	
meals, 20	B	Compliance (law, regulatory, finance)	Accounting, Per Diem, Gov. Rates	
travel, 20, 25	B	Compliance (law, regulatory, finance)	Accounting, Per Diem, Gov. Rates	
OCONUS, 12, 18	B	Government Contracting (DoD)	Accounting, Per Diem, Gov. Rates	
overseas, 4	B	Government Contracting (DoD)	Accounting, Per Diem, Gov. Rates	
DCAA, 7, 8, 13	B	Compliance (law, regulatory, finance)	Auditing & Accounting	
DCMA, 13	B	Compliance (law, regulatory, finance)	Auditing & Accounting	
Defense Contract Audit Agency, 13	B	Compliance (law, regulatory, finance)	Auditing & Accounting	
Defense Contracting Management Agency, 13	B	Compliance (law, regulatory, finance)	Auditing & Accounting	
Defense Financial Accounting Service, 14	B	Compliance (law, regulatory, finance)	Auditing & Accounting	
Defense Logistics Support Services, 15	B	Compliance (law, regulatory, finance)	Auditing & Accounting	
Donations, 14	B	Compliance (law, regulatory, finance)	Auditing & Accounting	
entertainment, 16	B	Compliance (law, regulatory, finance)	Auditing & Accounting	
expenditure, 10	B	Compliance (law, regulatory, finance)	Auditing & Accounting	
expense, 10, 19	B	Compliance (law, regulatory, finance)	Auditing & Accounting	

Topic (Code) With Interview "specific" Page	Interview #	CODE MAIN THEMES	SECONDARY MAIN THEMES	NOTES
Federal Acquisition Register, 2, 3	B	Compliance (law, regulatory, finance)	Auditing & Accounting	
Federal Acquisition Regulation, 8, 16	B	Compliance (law, regulatory, finance)	Auditing & Accounting	
Finance, 7, 10, 26, 28	2	Compliance (law, regulatory, finance)	Auditing & Accounting	
fines, 19	B	Compliance (law, regulatory, finance)	Auditing & Accounting	
General & Administrative (G&A), 19	B	Compliance (law, regulatory, finance)	Auditing & Accounting	
gifts, 17	B	Compliance (law, regulatory, finance)	Auditing & Accounting	
OFCCP, 3	B	Compliance (law, regulatory, finance)	Auditing & Accounting	
Office of Federal Contract Compliance Programs, 3	B	Compliance (law, regulatory, finance)	Auditing & Accounting	
parties, 19	B	Compliance (law, regulatory, finance)	Auditing & Accounting	
proper audit trails, 21	B	Compliance (law, regulatory, finance)	Auditing & Accounting	
unallowable, 10, 16, 19, 25	B	Compliance (law, regulatory, finance)	Auditing & Accounting	
benefits, 2, 4, 6, 7	B	Benefits and Compensation	Benefits and Compensation	
compensation, 2, 4, 6	B	Benefits and Compensation	Benefits and Compensation	
Fringe Benefits, 21	B	Benefits and Compensation	Benefits and Compensation	
premium pay, 18	B	Benefits and Compensation	Benefits and Compensation	
raises, 2	2	Benefits and Compensation	Benefits and Compensation	
salary, 6, 9, 11, 12, 18, 21	B	Benefits and Compensation	Benefits and Compensation	

Topic (Code) With Interview "specific" Page	Interview #	CODE MAIN THEMES	SECONDARY MAIN THEMES	NOTES
promotion, 20, 21	B	Company or Security Clearance specific	Benefits and Compensation	
classifications, 11, 18	B	Compensation & Recruiting	Benefits and Compensation	
overtime, 12, 18, 19, 24	B	Compliance (law, regulatory, finance)	Benefits and Compensation	
pay, 4, 10, 14, 18, 19, 24	B	Compliance (law, regulatory, finance)	Benefits and Compensation	
payroll, 7, 9	B	Compliance (law, regulatory, finance)	Benefits and Compensation	
policies, 10, 15, 20, 26	B	Company or Security Clearance specific	Company internal policies	
procedures, 20, 26	B	Company or Security Clearance specific	Company internal policies	
process, 6, 20, 22, 23, 24	B	Company or Security Clearance specific	Company internal policies	
rules, 20	B	Company or Security Clearance specific	Company internal policies	
approval matrix, 11	B	Compliance (law, regulatory, finance)	Company internal policies	
alcohol policy, 10	B	Contract Compliance (mandated policies)	Company internal policies	
orientation, 2, 3, 6	B	Training & Development	Company internal policies	
training and development, 5, 6	B	Training & Development	Company internal policies	
training, 2, 4, 5, 6, 7, 16, 17, 25	B	Training & Development	Company internal policies	
badges, 21	B	Security (DoD) Clearances or worksite security	Contract Job Requirement	
clearances, 2, 4, 8, 21, 22, 23	B	Security (DoD) Clearances or worksite security	Contract Job Requirement	
secret, 21, 22	B	Security Clearance Related (DoD)	Contract Job Requirement	

Topic (Code) With Interview "specific" Page	Interview #	CODE MAIN THEMES	SECONDARY MAIN THEMES	NOTES
security clearances, 21	B	Security Clearance Related (DoD)	Contract Job Requirement	
audit, 5, 6, 13, 21, 24, 26	B	Compliance (law, regulatory, finance)	Contract Oversight	
floor checks, 13	B	Compliance (law, regulatory, finance)	Contract Oversight	
Civilian Agency Acquisition Council (CAAC)	O	Federal Acquisition Regulation (FAR), published as Chapter 1 of Title 48 of the Code of Federal Regulations	Contract Oversight	Provided under (joint) Secretary of Defense, Admin. Of Genl. Services Administration, Admin. Of NASA, Defense Acquisition Regulatory Council (DARC) and Civilian Agency Acquisition Council (CAAC).
Defense Acquisition Regulatory Council (DARC)	O	Federal Acquisition Regulation (FAR), published as Chapter 1 of Title 48 of the Code of Federal Regulations	Contract Oversight	Provided under (joint) Secretary of Defense, Admin. Of Genl. Services Administration, Admin. Of NASA, Defense Acquisition Regulatory Council (DARC) and Civilian Agency Acquisition Council (CAAC).
Title 48, Code of Federal Regulations	O	Federal Acquisition Regulation (FAR), published as Chapter 1 of Title 48 of the Code of Federal Regulations	Contract Oversight	Provided under (joint) Secretary of Defense, Admin. Of Genl. Services Administration, Admin. Of NASA, Defense Acquisition Regulatory Council (DARC) and Civilian Agency Acquisition Council (CAAC).
products, 2	B	Company or Security Clearance specific	Contract Requirements	Provided to client
acquisition, 2	B	Compliance (law, regulatory, finance)	Contract Requirements	
contract law, 2	B	Compliance (law, regulatory, finance)	Contract Requirements	
contract line item number, 11	B	Compliance (law, regulatory, finance)	Contract Requirements	
deliverables, 14	B	Compliance (law, regulatory, finance)	Contract Requirements	
delivery orders, 13, 14	B	Compliance (law, regulatory, finance)	Contract Requirements	
drug policy, 10	B	Compliance (law, regulatory, finance)	Contract Requirements	

Topic (Code) With Interview "specific" Page	Interview #	CODE MAIN THEMES	SECONDARY MAIN THEMES	NOTES
E-Verify, 3	B	Compliance (law, regulatory, finance)	Contract Requirements	
line item, 11, 24	B	Contracts, Proposals, Compliance	Contract Requirements	
abilities, 2	B	Recruiting (requirements for compliance hiring)	Contract Requirements	
access, 24	B	Security (DoD) Clearances	Contract Requirements	
cost to contract, 14	B	Compliance (law, regulatory, finance)	Contracting - Government	
Federal Acquisition, 17	B	Compliance (law, regulatory, finance)	Contracting - Government	
government contracting, 1, 2, 3, 4, 8, 10, 15, 18, 25, 26	B	Compliance (law, regulatory, finance)	Contracting - Government	
government contractors, 3, 4, 5, 15	B	Compliance (law, regulatory, finance)	Contracting - Government	
Laws	O	Compliance (law, regulatory, finance)	Contracting - Government	
Posters	O	Compliance (law, regulatory, finance)	Contracting - Government	
bids and proposals, 11	B	Contract Compliance (mandated policies)	Contracting - Government	
Contract Administrative Services, 11	B	Contracts, Proposals, Compliance	Contracting - Government	
contract administrator, 11, 19	B	Contracts, Proposals, Compliance	Contracting - Government	
contract officer, 20	B	Contracts, Proposals, Compliance	Contracting - Government	
Contracting Officer, 10	B	Contracts, Proposals, Compliance	Contracting - Government	
contractor, 3, 4, 10, 14, 15, 16, 23, 24, 26	B	Contracts, Proposals, Compliance	Contracting - Government	

Topic (Code) With Interview "specific" Page	Interview #	CODE MAIN THEMES	SECONDARY MAIN THEMES	NOTES
contracts, 6, 11, 14, 16, 18	B	Contracts, Proposals, Compliance	Contracting - Government	
defense contractors, 3	B	Contracts, Proposals, Compliance	Contracting - Government	
proposal, 11, 14	B	Contracts, Proposals, Compliance	Contracting - Government	
sub-contracts, 24	B	Contracts, Proposals, Compliance	Contracting - Government	
Office of Contract Compliance Programs	O	EEOC job opportunities; anti-kickback compensation	Contracting - Government	
Department of Defense, 2, 8	B	FAR - Contract Regulatory Law	Contracting - Government	
Office of Small Business Programs	O	Small, disadvantaged & small women-owned business, minority colleges/ universities	Contracting - Government	
job classification, 18	B	Benefits and Compensation	EEOC, AAP, Compensation	
job families, 18	B	Benefits and Compensation	EEOC, AAP, Compensation	
labor categories, 18	B	Benefits and Compensation	EEOC, AAP, Compensation	
labor classification, 18	B	Benefits and Compensation	EEOC, AAP, Compensation	
Department of Labor, 3	B	Compliance (law, regulatory, finance)	EEOC, AAP, Compensation	
EEOC, 3	B	Compliance (law, regulatory, finance)	EEOC, AAP, Compensation	
publicly traded, 5	B	Compliance (law, regulatory, finance)	Ethics	
Sarbanes-Oxley, 5, 26	B	Compliance (law, regulatory, finance)	Ethics	
ethics training, 16, 17	1	Training & Development	Ethics	
prostitution, 5	B	Training & Development	Ethics	
ethics, 2, 4, 5, 6, 10, 14, 16, 17	B	Training & Development	Ethics	

Topic (Code) With Interview "specific" Page	Interview #	CODE MAIN THEMES	SECONDARY MAIN THEMES	NOTES
HR, 1, 2, 3, 5, 6, 7, 8, 9, 10, 11, 12, 14, 16, 17, 18, 20, 21, 25, 26	B	HR Capabilities (overall) - KSA's	General HR	
Drug screen, 14, 15	B	Company mandated for contract compliance	Government Contracting Requirements	
Executive Orders	O	Compliance (law, regulatory, finance)	Government Contracting Requirements	
FAR, 8, 16, 17, 21	B	Compliance (law, regulatory, finance)	Government Contracting Requirements	
FLSA	O	Compliance (law, regulatory, finance)	Government Contracting Requirements	
Office of Contract Compliance Programs (OFCCP)	O	Compliance (law, regulatory, finance)	Government Contracting Requirements	Random audits, surges of discrimination complaints, pressure from minority or community groups, construction industry, first time contractor pre-award review, EEO-1 with outliers
Executive Order 11246	O	Affirmative Action Plan (create)	Legal, Regulatory, and Exec. Orders	Create and annually update an Affirmative Action Plan for women and minorities.
Jobs for Veterans Act (JVA)	O	Affirmative Action Plan (create)	Legal, Regulatory, and Exec. Orders	Contractors must engage in affirmative action for disabled vets, vets w/ active duty in last 1-3 years, active duty w/ campaign badge, service medal veterans, VETS-100
prevailing wages, 20	B	Benefits and Compensation	Legal, Regulatory, and Exec. Orders	
Service Contract Act, 12, 21	B	Benefits and Compensation	Legal, Regulatory, and Exec. Orders	
compliance, 2, 3, 4, 13	B	Compliance (law, regulatory, finance)	Legal, Regulatory, and Exec. Orders	
Davis Bacon Act, 12	B	Compliance (law, regulatory, finance)	Legal, Regulatory, and Exec. Orders	

Topic (Code) With Interview "specific" Page	Interview #	CODE MAIN THEMES	SECONDARY MAIN THEMES	NOTES
Department of Labor's Office of Federal Contract Compliance Programs	O	Compliance (law, regulatory, finance)	Legal, Regulatory, and Exec. Orders	Definition of Applicant: 1) expressed an interest in employment via Internet (electronic portal), 2) employer seeks applicants for a unique position, 3) the individual possesses basic qualifications, and 4) the individual does not remove him/herself from consideration.
Executive Order 13201	O	Compliance (law, regulatory, finance)	Legal, Regulatory, and Exec. Orders	Government contractors and subcontractors with $100,000+ in contracts, 15+ EE's, inside USA borders, Poster - Notice of Employee Rights Concerning Payment of Union Dues
executive orders, 3, 19	B	Compliance (law, regulatory, finance)	Legal, Regulatory, and Exec. Orders	
regulations, 8, 20	B	Compliance (law, regulatory, finance)	Legal, Regulatory, and Exec. Orders	
wage determinations, 12, 13, 21	B	Compliance (law, regulatory, finance)	Legal, Regulatory, and Exec. Orders	
Section 503 of the Rehabilitation Act	O	Covers disabled workers	Legal, Regulatory, and Exec. Orders	
Rehabilitation Act of 1973	O	Federal contractors w/ $10,000+ in contracts	Legal, Regulatory, and Exec. Orders	
Drug-Free Workplace Act (1988)	O	Federal contractors w/ $100,000+ in contracts	Legal, Regulatory, and Exec. Orders	EE'rs must 'Certify' they have established a drug-free awareness program, publish, efforts to train, condition of employment on fed contract, penalties (drug tests not mandatory)
Vietnam Era Veteran's Readjustment Assistance Act (1974)	O	Federal contractors w/ $100,000+ in contracts	Legal, Regulatory, and Exec. Orders	File Fed. Contractor Veteran's Employment Report VETS-100 + have AAP in place.
Executive Order 11246 (1965)	O	Federal contractors w/ $50,000+ in contracts	Legal, Regulatory, and Exec. Orders	EEO-1 must be filed annually for those with 50+ EE"s

Topic (Code) With Interview "specific" Page	Interview #	CODE MAIN THEMES	SECONDARY MAIN THEMES	NOTES
Annual Reporting Forms	O	Federal contractors, 100+ employees, Contracts $100K+, Due each Sept 30th.	Legal, Regulatory, and Exec. Orders	EEO-1 (private business), EEO-2 (joint apprenticeship programs), EEO-2,A (unilateral apprenticeship programs), EEO-4 (state/local governments), EEO-5 (public/elementary & 2ndary schools), IPEDS (integrated post-secondary education data system [colleges/universities].
Foreign Corrupt Practices Act (FCPA), 1977	O	Firm doing business in foreign markets are prohibited from making corrupt payments to foreign officials to obtain/keep business.	Legal, Regulatory, and Exec. Orders	
Affirmative Action Plans (AAP)	O	Government contractors with $10,000+ for one or $50,000 in multiple contracts	Legal, Regulatory, and Exec. Orders	
Office of Safety and Health Administration (OSHA)	O	Minimum number of inspections annually for underground and surface mines.	Legal, Regulatory, and Exec. Orders	Part of the Mine Safety and Health Administration (MSHA) under the Department of Labor (US)
Fair Credit Reporting Act (FCRA)	O	Must obtain a signed release from applicant	Legal, Regulatory, and Exec. Orders	Investigations must be relevant to the job (e.g., no finance checks for a receptionist that doesn't handle cash)
Executive Order 11246	O	Record Retention	Legal, Regulatory, and Exec. Orders	Federal contractors must keep employment records for 2 years after an employment decision or creation of personnel record, whichever later
Rehabilitation Act of 1973	O	Record Retention	Legal, Regulatory, and Exec. Orders	Federal contractors must keep employment records for 2 years after an employment decision or creation of personnel record, whichever later
Vietnam Era Veteran's Readjustment Assistance Act (1974)	O	Record Retention	Legal, Regulatory, and Exec. Orders	Federal contractors must keep employment records for 2 years after an employment decision or creation of personnel record, whichever later

Topic (Code) With Interview "specific" Page	Interview #	CODE MAIN THEMES	SECONDARY MAIN THEMES	NOTES
Vietnam Era Veterans Readjustment Assistance Act (VEVRA)	O	Recruiting (reqs for compliance hiring)	Legal, Regulatory, and Exec. Orders	Contractors must post all job openings with appropriate local employment service office(s); VETS-100
Employee Polygraph Protection Act (EPPA)	O	Safety	Legal, Regulatory, and Exec. Orders	DoD - Security Cleared Personnel - contractors & employees performing intelligence functions
Whistleblowing	O	SOX - Section 806 (part of the False Claims Act of 1863)	Legal, Regulatory, and Exec. Orders	OSHA or SEC handles these charges
federal contractors	O	Specific and Additional Regulations, Law, Compliance	Legal, Regulatory, and Exec. Orders	
JPAS, 8, 23	B	Benefits and Compensation	Military Employee Benefits	
United States, 12	B	Company or Security Clearance specific	NA	
CONUS, 11, 12	B	Benefits and Compensation	Payroll, Wages, Accounting, Auditing, Taxes	Travel, Per Diem, Training Requirements
man-hours, 7, 8, 18	B	Benefits and Compensation	Payroll, Wages, Accounting, Auditing, Taxes	
minimum wage, 20	1	Benefits and Compensation	Payroll, Wages, Accounting, Auditing, Taxes	
accounting, 10	B	Compliance (law, regulatory, finance)	Payroll, Wages, Accounting, Auditing, Taxes	
Defense Logistics Support Services (DLSS), 15	B	Compliance (law, regulatory, finance)	Payroll, Wages, Accounting, Auditing, Taxes	
G&A, 19	B	Compliance (law, regulatory, finance)	Payroll, Wages, Accounting, Auditing, Taxes	
indirect, 14, 19	B	Compliance (law, regulatory, finance)	Payroll, Wages, Accounting, Auditing, Taxes	
interest, 17	B	Compliance (law, regulatory, finance)	Payroll, Wages, Accounting, Auditing, Taxes	
Pay / Payroll	O	Compliance (law, regulatory, finance)	Payroll, Wages, Accounting, Auditing, Taxes	

Topic (Code) With Interview "specific" Page	Interview #	CODE MAIN THEMES	SECONDARY MAIN THEMES	NOTES
project accounting, 20	B	Compliance (law, regulatory, finance)	Payroll, Wages, Accounting, Auditing, Taxes	
SCA, 4, 12, 13, 21	B	Compliance (law, regulatory, finance)	Payroll, Wages, Accounting, Auditing, Taxes	
Service Contract Act (1965)	O	Compliance (law, regulatory, finance)	Payroll, Wages, Accounting, Auditing, Taxes	
taxes, 9	B	Compliance (law, regulatory, finance)	Payroll, Wages, Accounting, Auditing, Taxes	
Time Card, 12	B	Compliance (law, regulatory, finance)	Payroll, Wages, Accounting, Auditing, Taxes	
timekeeping, 12	B	Compliance (law, regulatory, finance)	Payroll, Wages, Accounting, Auditing, Taxes	
timesheet changes, 24	B	Compliance (law, regulatory, finance)	Payroll, Wages, Accounting, Auditing, Taxes	
timesheet, 2, 7, 24, 25	B	Compliance (law, regulatory, finance)	Payroll, Wages, Accounting, Auditing, Taxes	
total time accounting, 25	B	Compliance (law, regulatory, finance)	Payroll, Wages, Accounting, Auditing, Taxes	
W-2, 9	B	Compliance (law, regulatory, finance)	Payroll, Wages, Accounting, Auditing, Taxes	
Walsh-Healy Public Contracts Act	O	Contractors w/ $10,000+ in contracts	Payroll, Wages, Accounting, Auditing, Taxes	Right to minimum wage for all hours worked, and time and a half for all hours worked over 40; specific types of EE's
electronic, 26	B	Documentation	Payroll, Wages, Accounting, Auditing, Taxes	
Executive Order 11246	O	Federal contractors w/ $10,000+ in contracts	Payroll, Wages, Accounting, Auditing, Taxes	Pay discrimination per EEOC
Equal Employment Opportunity (EEOC)	O	Federal contractors w/ $2,500+ in contracts	Payroll, Wages, Accounting, Auditing, Taxes	Prevailing Wages/Fringe Benefits
McNamara-O'Hara Service Contract Act (SCA)	O	Federal contractors w/ $2,500+ in contracts	Payroll, Wages, Accounting, Auditing, Taxes	Geographically specified wages, plus fringe benefits and/or wages
Davis-Bacon	O	Payroll, salary, compensation	Payroll, Wages, Accounting, Auditing, Taxes	Prevailing Wages/Fringe Benefits

Topic (Code) With Interview "specific" Page	Interview #	CODE MAIN THEMES	SECONDARY MAIN THEMES	NOTES
Fringe Benefits	O	Payroll, salary, compensation	Payroll, Wages, Accounting, Auditing, Taxes	
hours, 2, 7, 8, 12, 18, 19, 24	B	Timesheet, Documentation, Hours on Contract	Payroll, Wages, Accounting, Auditing, Taxes	
checks and balances, 5, 6, 7	B	Ethics, Quality Assurance, Training	Quality Assurance - T&D	
background check, 21, 22, 23	B	Company or Security Clearance specific	Recruiting Specific	
advertising, 10, 14	B	Compliance (law, regulatory, finance)	Recruiting Specific	
verification, 9	B	Compliance (law, regulatory, finance)	Recruiting Specific	
requisition, 3	B	Recruiting (reqs for compliance hiring)	Recruiting specific	
certificate, 4, 16	B	Recruiting (requirements for compliance hiring)	Recruiting Specific	
licenses, 4	B	Recruiting (requirements for compliance hiring)	Recruiting Specific	
qualifications, 4	B	Recruiting (requirements for compliance hiring)	Recruiting Specific	
recruiting, 2, 3, 4, 6	B	Recruiting (requirements for compliance hiring)	Recruiting Specific	
recruitment, 10, 13	B	Recruiting (requirements for compliance hiring)	Recruiting Specific	
confidential, 21, 22	B	Security (DoD) Clearances	Recruiting Specific	
Contract Work Hours & Safety Standards Act (CWH-SSA)	O	Benefits and Compensation	Safety, OSHA, Workers Comp	
health	O	Compliance (law, regulatory, finance)	Safety, OSHA, Workers Comp	
OSHA, 3, 6, 7	B	Compliance (law, regulatory, finance)	Safety, OSHA, Workers Comp	

Topic (Code) With Interview "specific" Page	Interview #	CODE MAIN THEMES	SECONDARY MAIN THEMES	NOTES
safety	O	Compliance (law, regulatory, finance)	Safety, OSHA, Workers Comp	
workers compensation, 3, 6	B	Compliance (law, regulatory, finance)	Safety, OSHA, Workers Comp	
hazardous, 4	B	Training & Development	Safety, OSHA, Workers Comp	
annual training, 16	B	Contract Compliance (mandated policies)	Training and Development	
new hire, 2, 3, 7, 15	B	Recruiting (requirements for compliance hiring)	Training and Development	
Human Trafficking, 5	2	Training & Development	Training and Development	

References / Bibliography

Angeri, M. J. (2000). Evaluating interpretive inquiry: Reviewing the validity debate and opening the dialogue. *Qualitative Health Research, 10*(3), 378-395. doi: 10.1177/104973230001000308

Bessett, G. (2004). *Involving the Community: A Guide to Participatory Development Communication*. Ottawa: International Development Research Centre.

Brooks, S., & Howie, L. (2008). Therapist as researcher: Using heuristic methodology in a study of spoken language in a therapeutic relationship. *Gestalt Journal of Australia and New Zealand, 5*(1), 13-31.

Campbell, D. T., & Russo, M. J. (1999). *Social Experimentation*. Thousand Oaks, CA: Sage.

Caravatti, M.-L. (1996). The role of governments in the development of human resources training for employability. *Canada -- United States Law Journal 22*, 37-44.

CEBS designation - about the program. Retrieved September 27, 2010, from http://www.ifebp.org/CEBSDesignation/Overview/

Cortez, T. (2007, July). Of seasoned HR professionals: What types of credentials would you see necessary for future HR business partners? , from http://www.linkedin.com/answers/hiring-human-resources/staffing-recruiting/HRH_SFF/73445-9231735?searchIdx=6&sik=1265401064555&goback=%2Easr_1_1265401064555

Dick, R. (2006, Dec.). Action research literature 2004-2006: Themes and trends. *Action Research, 4*(4), 439-458. doi: 10.1177/1476750306070105

Elswick, J. (2001, Nov.). Letter perfect: Experts certification programs advise benefit professionals to get a comma after their names. *Employee Benefit News*. Retrieved from http://www.lexisnexis.com.proxy.lib.odu.edu/us/lnacademic

Federal Acquisition Regulation (FAR). (2010). Washington, DC: U.S. General Services Administration (GSA) Retrieved from http://www.gsa.gov/portal/content/101126.

Fine, M., & Torre, M. E. (2006). Intimate details: Participatory action research in prison. *Action Research, 4*(3), 253-269. doi: 10.1177/1476750306066801

Frequently asked questions. (2010, Sept.). Washington, DC: Small Business Administration, Office of Advocacy.

Gibson, P. (2009). *U.S. Master Human Resources Guide*. Chicago, IL: CCH, Paul Gibson, A Wolters Kluwer Company.

Hays, D. G., Prosek, E. A., & McLeod, A. L. (2010, Winter). A mixed methodological analysis of the role of culture in the clinical decision-making process *Journal of Counseling and Development, 88*(1), 114-121.

Hays, D. G., & Singh, A. A. (2011a). *Qualitative Inquiry in Clinical and Educational Settings*. New York, NY: Guilford.

Hays, D. G., & Singh, A. A. (2011b). Qualitative research paradigms and traditions *Qualitative Inquiry in Clinical and Educational Settings*. New York, NY: Guilford.

Hoyt, B. (2010, Aug. 17). We the people: Be on guard against corporate takeover, *Crossville Chronicle*, p. 1. Retrieved from http://crossville-chronicle.com/opinion/x743764296/WE-THE-PEOPLE-Be-on-guard-against-corporate-takeover

HRCI. (2010). Human resources institute overview, 2010, from http://hrci.org/

Human Resources Management Guide: Your Essential Compliance Resource. (2010). Neenah: Wi: J.J. Keller & Associates.

Human resources, training, and labor relations managers and specialists report (2010-2011). In Occupational Outlook Advocacy (Ed.), *Occupational Outlook Handbook, 2010-11 Edition*. Washington, DC: Bureau of Labor Statistics, U.S. Department of Labor.

Kidd, S. A., & Kral, M. J. (2005). Practicing participatory action research. *Journal of Counseling Psychology, 52*(2), 187-195. doi: 10.1037/0022-0167.52.2.187

Mandal, K. (2008, Feb.). How useful is a PHR Certification for HR Professionals? Retrieved from http://www.linkedin.com/answers/hiring-human-resources/staffing-recruiting/HRH_SFF/177370-4855570?searchIdx=33&sik=1265401064555&goback=%2Easr_4_1265401064555

McManus, D. (2010, July 18). Another kind of depression: Pervasive gloom will prolong the pain of the great recession, *OregonLive.com*, pp. 1-3. Retrieved from http://blog.oregonlive.com/opinion_impact/print.html?entry=/2010/07/another_kind_of_depression_per.html

Meisinger, S. (2004, April). Certification is worth the effort...and then some. *HRMagazine*, Editorial - from the President.

Military industrial complex. (2010). Retrieved September 24, 2010, 2010, from http://www.sourcewatch.org/index.php?title=Military-industrial_complex

Moustakas, C. (1994). *Phenomenological Research Methods*. Thousand Oaks, CA: Sage Publications, Inc.

Nadler, D., & Berger, J. R. (2009, Jan.). President Obama heralds change for government contracting. *The Government Contractor, Information and Analysis on Legal Aspects of Procurement, 51*(3), 1-5.

Newell, E. (2010, June). Lawmakers criticize growth of federal workers. *Government Executive*, 1. Retrieved from http://www.govexec.com/story_page_pf.cfm?articleid=45426&printerfriendlyvers=1

Noble, E. D., Aaron P. (2005, August). *Determining the effectiveness of the international public management association for human resources certified professional certification program in assisting HR managers in performing the responsibilities of their job*. PhD. Dissertation, University of North Carolina, Chapel Hill. (AAT 3164023)

Obama orders overhaul of government contracting. (2009). YouTube.com.

Our history. Retrieved from http://www.ifebp.org/AboutUs/Our+History/

Pane, D. M., & Salmon-Florida, A. (2009, Winter). The experience of isolation in alternative education: A heuristic research study. *Western Journal of Black Studies, 33*(4), 282-292.

Patton, C. (2010). HR technology: Today and tomorrow. [Article]. *University Business, 13*(7), 57-58.

Patton, M. Q. (1997). *Utilization-Focused Evaluation: The New Century Text* (3rd ed.). Thousand Oaks, CA: Sage.

Patton, M. Q. (2002). Designing qualitative studies. In C. D. Laughton (Ed.),

Qualitative Research & Evaluation Methods (3rd ed., pp. 230-242). Thousand Oaks, CA: Sage.

Rivera, L., Alvarado, J., Roberts, P., & Burns, A. (2002, Sept. 18). History of the defense industry. University of New Mexico, NM.

Rynes, S. L., Colbert, Amy E., Brown, Kenneth G. (2002, Summer). HR professionals' beliefs about effective human resource practices: Correspondence between research and practice. *Human Resource Management, 41(2)*.

Sandelowski, M. (1986). The problem of rigor in qualitative research. *Advances in Nursing Science, 8*(3), 27-37.

Sherk, J. (2010, June-a). Unemployment remains high because job creation has yet to recover *Backgrounder on Labor* (pp. 1-12). Washington, DC: The Heritage Foundation.

Sherk, J. (2010, June-b). Unemployment remains high because job creation has yet to recover (Vol. 2420, pp. 1-12). Washington, DC: The Heritage Foundation.

SHRM's mission and history. (2010). Retrieved from http://www.shrm.org/about/history/Pages/default.aspx

Society of Human Resource Management Learning System. (2010). (2010 ed.). Alexandria, VA: Society of Human Resources Management (SHRM).

Stephenson, S., & Loewenthal, D. (2006, Nov.). The effect on counseling/psychotherapy practice of an absent father in therapist's childhood: A heuristic study. *Psychodynamic Practice, 12*(4), 435-452. doi: 10.1080/14753630600958304

Stoecker, R. (1999, Feb.). Are academics irrelevant?: Roles for scholars in participatory research. *American Behavioral Scientist, 42*(5), 840-854. doi: 10.1177/00027649921954561

Stoecker, R. (2005). *Research methods for community change: a project-based approach* (1 ed.). Thousand Oaks, CA: Sage Publications, Inc.

Stoecker, R., & Bonacich, E. (1992). Why participatory research? Guest editors' introduction. *The American Sociologist, 23*(4), 5-13. doi: 10.1007/BF02691927

U.S. Federal Contractor Registration (CCR). (2010). Retrieved from http://uscontractorregistration.com/

U.S. Small Business Administration (SBA). (2010). Retrieved from http://www.sba.gov/

Wertz, F. J. (2005a). Phenomenological research methods for counseling psychology. *Journal of Counseling Psychology, 52*(2), 167-177. doi: 10.1037/0022-0167.52.2.167

Wertz, F. J. (2005b). Phenomenological research methods for counseling psychology. *Journal of Counseling Psychology, 52*(2), 167-177. doi: 10.1037/0022-0167.52.2.167

What is certification preparation. Retrieved from http://www.hrci.org/about/

Yang, Y.-F. (2008). The roles of human resources, information technology, and marketing knowledge of capabilities in performance: An extension of the resources-based theory perspective. [Article]. *Social Behavior & Personality: An International Journal, 36*(9), 1269-1282. doi: 10.2224/sbp.2008.36.9.1269

Yoon, J. K., & Sundar, S. S. (2010, April). Heuristic versus systematic processing of specialist versus generalist sources in online media. *Human Communication Research, 36*(2), 103-124. doi: 10.1111/j.1468-2958.2010.01370.x

Zulauf, C. A., Johansen, K. J., Kusy, M. E., Rouda, R., Rowden, R. W., & Turner, B. S. (1996). *HRD & business outcomes.* Paper presented at the Academy of Human Resources Development, 1996 Conference, Minneapolis, MN.

ABOUT THE AUTHOR

Dawn D. Boyer, Ph.D. completed her Doctor of Philosophy in Education (Occupational & Technical Studies, with a concentration in Training & Development in Human Resources) from Old Dominion University in Norfolk, VA in 2013. Her dissertation is entitled, 'Competencies of Human Resources Practitioners within the Government Contracting Industry,' which identified unique KSAs for Human Resources Managers working for federal level government contracting companies. This groundbreaking research is the impetus upon her textbook guide for Human Resources Professionals in Government Contracting, currently in the works.

She has been an entrepreneur and business owner for 14+ years, currently in her consulting firm, D. Boyer Consulting, based in Richmond (Henrico County), VA, and servicing clients internationally. Her background experience is 24+ years in the Human Resources field, of which 11 years are within the federal defense contracting industry.

Dr. Boyer's experience in federal (defense) contracting as a Human Resources Director or Senior Manager has provided her insight, experience, practice, and capabilities to perform within this industry, as well as instruct others to abilities needed in middle-management or executive human resource roles.

Dr. Boyer currently works with job and new career seekers to write Search Engine Optimized resumes for increased visibility to recruiters – getting the candidates past the recruiting 'firewall' and interviewed for faster hires and job placement. Her tech-based knowledge of how the ATS software systems work help job seekers in structuring a resume for recruiters' Boolean search queries. Her SEO coding within resume is so unique, no other resume writers offer this service.

She additionally assists academics and writers publish their works or manuscripts as a third-party publisher – DBC Publishing. She also assists business owners develop their brand and marketing plans within social media marketing, planning, and management.

She is the author of over 145 books on the topics of genealogy, family lineage, women and gender studies, business, and career search practice, quotes for self-improvement and motivation (2,000+ /3,000+ series), and her 'Interview with an Artist' series (three artists in the series to date). All her books are listed on her Amazon author's page at:

https://www.amazon.com/author/dawnboyer.

Dr. Boyer has been a member of LinkedIn since 2004 (a few months after beta version released) and has developed a rich profile for consistent and constant communications to ~12,600+ connections. Her clients call her 'The Queen of LinkedIn.'

She may be reached via her business website:

http://DBoyerConsulting.com

or by email:

Dawn.Boyer@DBoyerConsulting.com

CURRICULUM VITAE

DAWN D. BOYER, Ph.D.

B.F.A., M.Ad.Ed., CDR, CIR, LSS - Green Belt

- 24+ years, HR, Employee Relations, Recruiting, Training, Development, Presentations, Benefits/Compensation, Analysis/Auditing, and Employment Law/ Practices
- 13+ years, Entrepreneur, Business Owner, Business Partner
- 11+ years, Federal Defense Contractors (SBA 8(a), HUB Zone, Service Disabled Veteran Owned Business, Woman Owned, and Alaskan Native Corporation [ANC])
- 11+ years, Federal / Government Contracts Employment Issues and Laws
- 8+ years, Teaching, Training and Curriculum Development in business, information technology, and Human Resources in proprietary and public educational institutions
- 7+ years, Contracts, Negotiations, and Insurance Benefits Administration
- 3+ years, Graduate Teaching Assistant (GTA) for Undergraduate Studies

EMPLOYMENT HISTORY

08/10 - present, Resume Writing Subject Matter Expert, Social Media Management Consultant, Editing & Publishing (dba DBC Publishing), D. Boyer Consulting, Virginia Beach and Richmond, VA

12/15 – 06/16, Adjunct Professor, Art Institute of Virginia Beach, VA

06/15 – present, Reviewer/Editor, Academic Publications

08/09 – 12/12, Adjunct Instructor & Doctoral Graduate Teaching Assistant, Old Dominion University, Norfolk, VA

06/07 – 09/17, Vice President / HR Director, Business Development, and Social Media Manager
Monster Clean, Carpet, Oriental Rug & Upholstery Cleaning, Virginia Beach, VA

11/07 – 03/09, Director, Human Resources & Ethics Compliance
Chenega Advanced Solutions & Engineering, LLC, Norfolk, VA

05/05 – 11/07, Senior Corporate Recruiting Manager, Zel Technologies, LLC (ZelTech), Hampton, VA

01/03 – 04/05, Human Resources Manager (Corporate Specialist), AMSEC LLC (Corp HQ's) (a LLC between SAIC & Northrop Grumman Newport News Shipbuilding), Virginia Beach, VA (Corporate HQ's), (Subsidiary companies: Egan McAllister & Associates (EMA), PMI, M. Rosenblatt & Son, Inc., etc.)

03/01 – 01/03, AMSEC Human Resources Manager, LLC (IMEG / SETS Group)

07/95 – 01/01, Human Resources Manager, Norfolk Warehouse Mgmt. / The Taylor Cos., Norfolk, VA

12/94 - 07/95, Human Resources Creative Generalist, Metro Information Services, Inc., Va. Beach, VA

FORMAL EDUCATION

Doctor of Philosophy (PhD), Old Dominion University, Norfolk, VA; *Occupational and Technical Studies (Science, Technology, Engineering & Math in Professional Studies (STEMPS); concentration in Training & Development in Human Resources; GPA: 3.65*

Masters Degree in Education, Virginia Commonwealth University, Richmond, VA (1989), Adult Education - Human Resources, Training & Development, Personnel, and Staffing; GPA: 3.67

Bachelors Degree in Fine Art, Advertising, and Graphic Illustration, Radford University, Radford, VA (1983); Graphic Advertising & Illustration, Fine Art, and Art History; GPA: 3.25

Follow the Author on Social Media Platforms

D. Boyer Consulting

DBoyerConsulting.com

Join her 12,600+ connections on LinkedIn:

www.linkedin.com/in/DawnBoyer

Amazon Author Page:

www.amazon.com/author/dawnboyer

Review Author's books:

www.shelfari.com/DawnDeniseBoyer

Twitter at:

www.Twitter.com/Dawn_Boyer

YouTube Channel:

www.youtube.com/user/DawnDeniseBoyer

Interested in publishing your own academic essays, projects, or books? Contact the author for publishing project estimates, consulting, and assistance:

Dawn.Boyer@me.com

www.DBoyerConsulting.com

ABOUT THE BOOK

This book and its content is derived from the Ph.D. cohort, required-curriculum class for Education Foundations 814: Qualitative Research in Education, taught by Dr. Danica G. Hays, in the Fall Semester of 2010.

The project was to create a foundation upon which to design the Ph.D.' student's dissertation, and/or provide a stepping-stone foundation upon which to determine the best research methodologies for the student's final prospectus and dissertation. The initial dissertation research study was to be qualitative, but during development of the proposed prospectus and study, it was determined that a blend of both qualitative and quantitative methods would be best for the final study.

The results of the Qualitative Research in Education class provided this final project write-up, with literature review and bibliography, and is provided here in its description entirety, with exception of the anonymous participants' details.

www.ingramcontent.com/pod-product-compliance
Lightning Source LLC
Chambersburg PA
CBHW060852050426
42453CB00008B/950